HOW THINGS
WORK
VEHICLES
Coloring Book

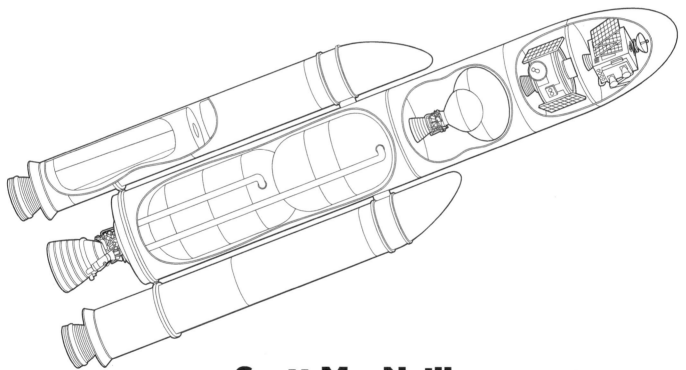

Scott MacNeill

DOVER PUBLICATIONS, INC.
Mineola, New York

Bibliographical Note

How Things Work: Vehicles Coloring Book is a new work, first
published by Dover Publications, Inc., in 2013.

International Standard Book Number

ISBN-13: 978-0-486-49221-6
ISBN-10: 0-486-49221-4

Manufactured in the United States by LSC Communications
49221404   2017
www.doverpublications.com

HOW THINGS
WORK
VEHICLES
Coloring Book

AIRPLANE

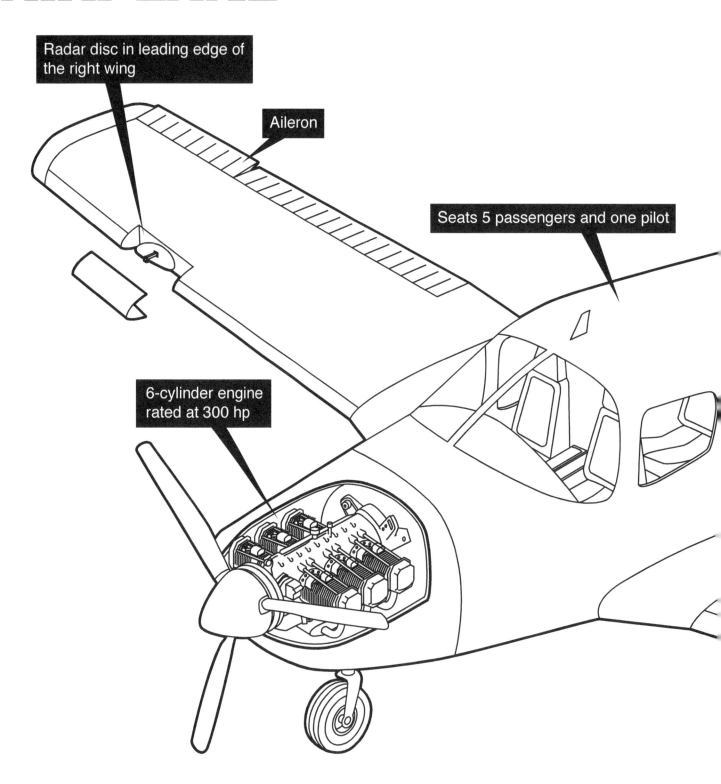

Radar disc in leading edge of the right wing

Aileron

Seats 5 passengers and one pilot

6-cylinder engine rated at 300 hp

SINGLE ENGINE PROP PLANE

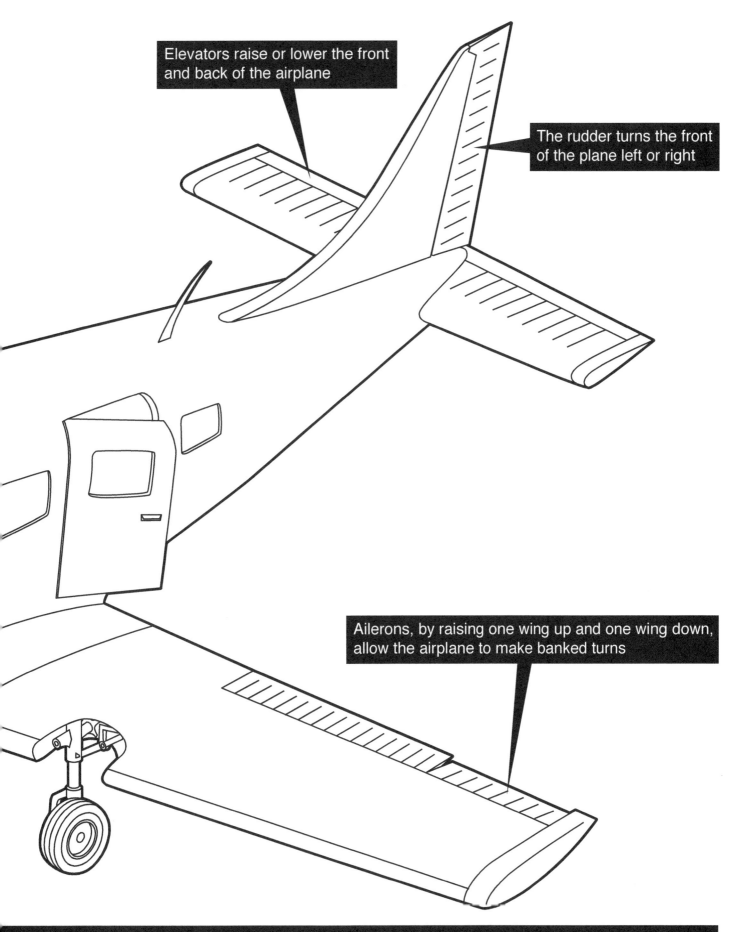

Elevators raise or lower the front and back of the airplane

The rudder turns the front of the plane left or right

Ailerons, by raising one wing up and one wing down, allow the airplane to make banked turns

A popular style of an all-metal fixed-wing aircrafts, for personal and small business usage with a cruise speed of 190 mph and a range of 1,000 miles.

AMBULANCE

Compartments containing medical supplies to cover almost every possible emergency

High-powered lights to help Illuminate the scene

Portable folding stretcher

A modern van-based ambulance designed to respond to medical emergencies

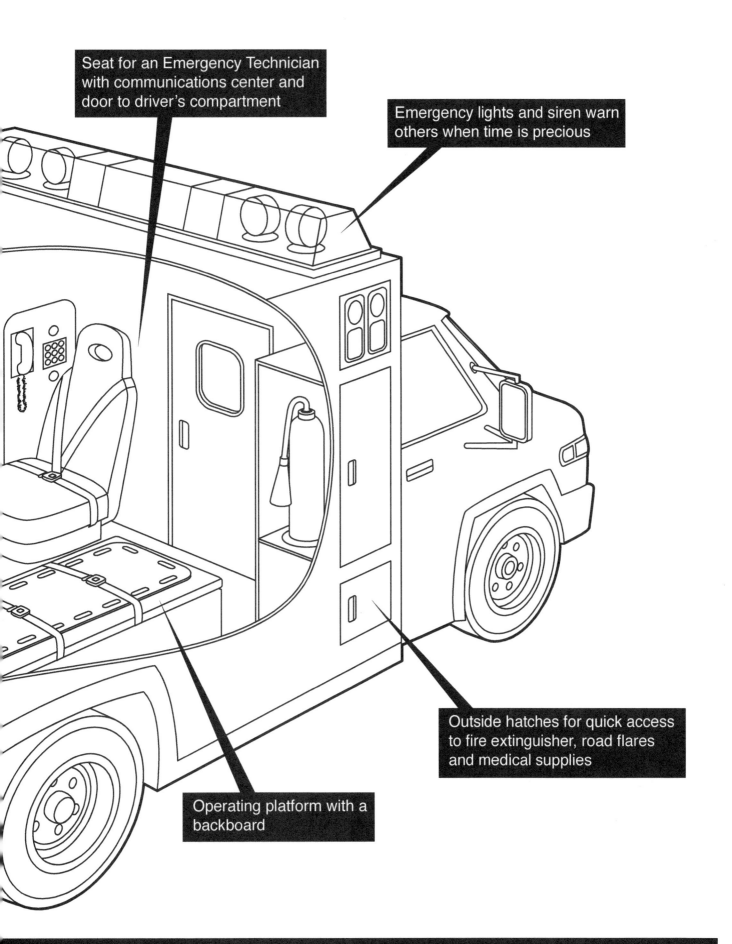

Seat for an Emergency Technician with communications center and door to driver's compartment

Emergency lights and siren warn others when time is precious

Outside hatches for quick access to fire extinguisher, road flares and medical supplies

Operating platform with a backboard

SAVING LIVES EVERYDAY

THE BACKHOE

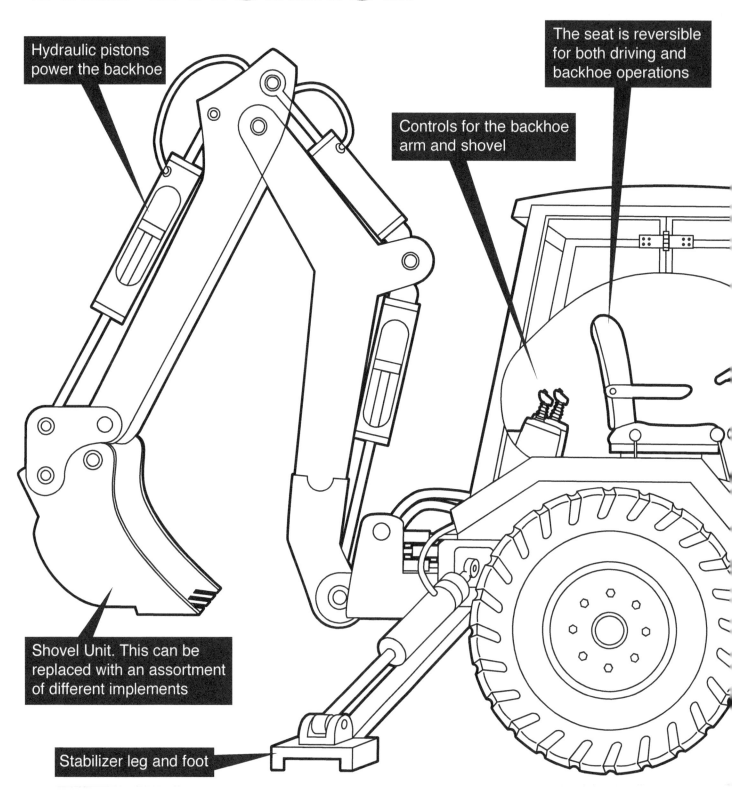

Hydraulic pistons power the backhoe

Controls for the backhoe arm and shovel

The seat is reversible for both driving and backhoe operations

Shovel Unit. This can be replaced with an assortment of different implements

Stabilizer leg and foot

TRACTOR WITH FRONT END LOADER

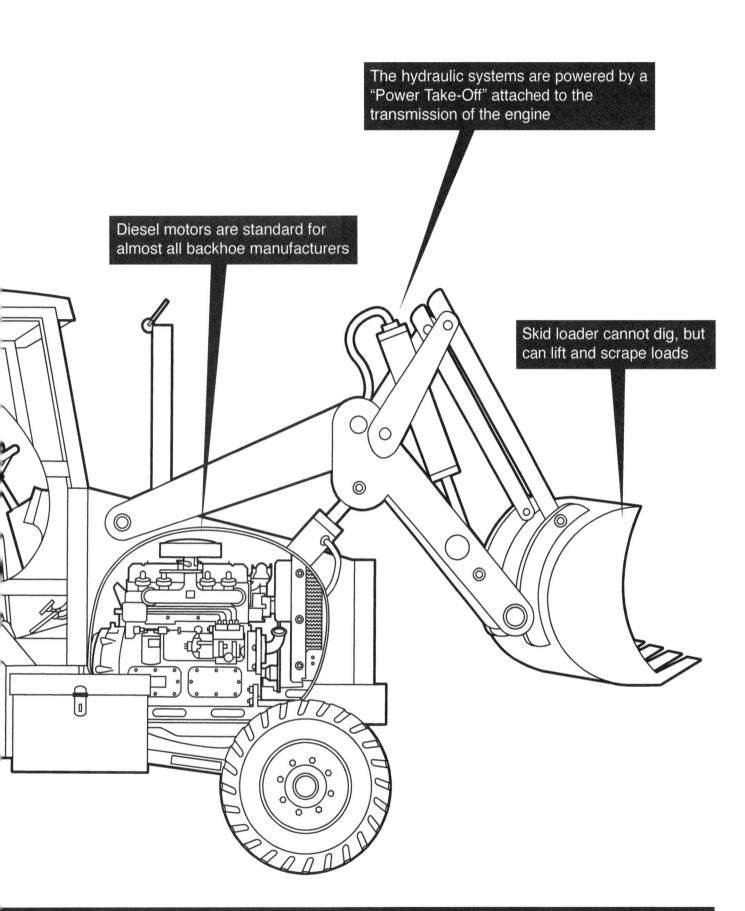

The hydraulic systems are powered by a "Power Take-Off" attached to the transmission of the engine

Diesel motors are standard for almost all backhoe manufacturers

Skid loader cannot dig, but can lift and scrape loads

A backhoe is actually the digging shovel and arm unit mounted in the back of a tractor. Normally found with a front bucket, also called a a skid loader, mounted at the front of the tractor.

THE BIGGEST TRUCK

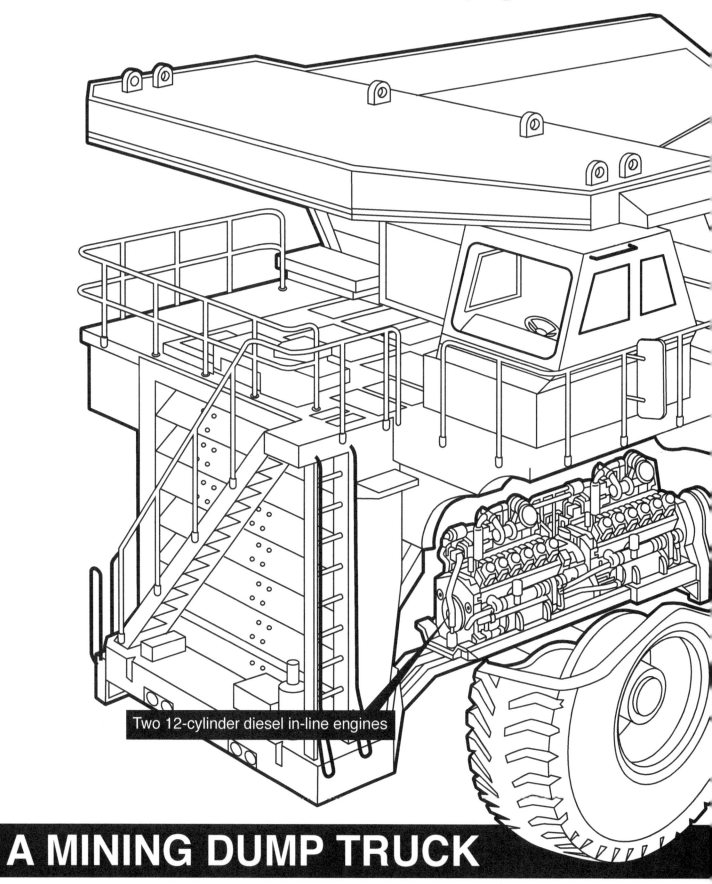

Two 12-cylinder diesel in-line engines

A MINING DUMP TRUCK

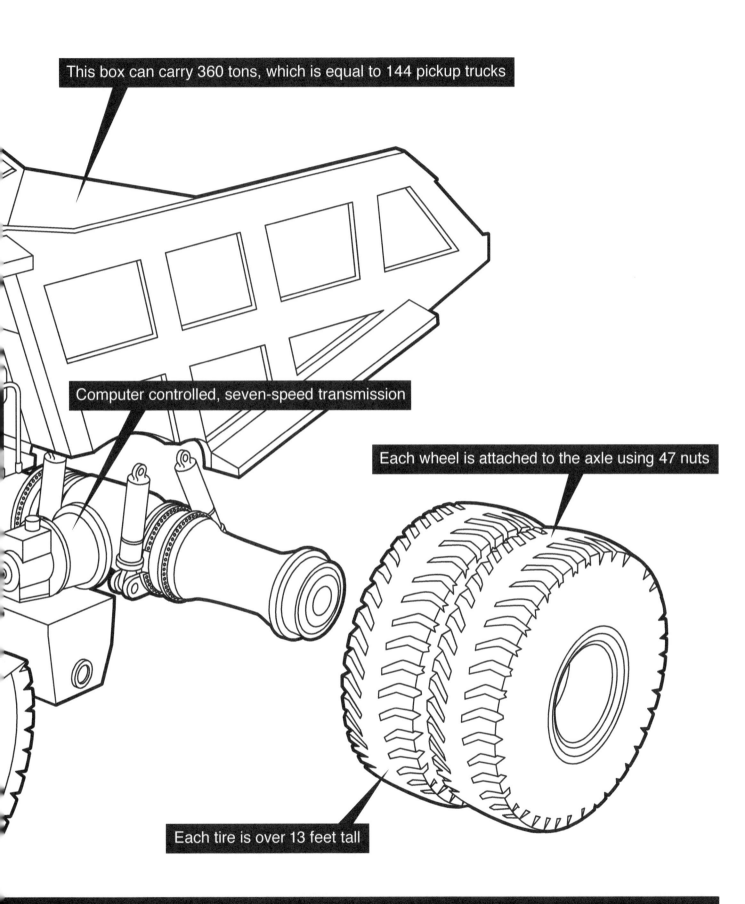

This box can carry 360 tons, which is equal to 144 pickup trucks

Computer controlled, seven-speed transmission

Each wheel is attached to the axle using 47 nuts

Each tire is over 13 feet tall

Each truck can require 12 to 13 semi-trailer trucks to deliver the truck in pieces to the work site, where it is assembled by a special team. Top speed while fully loaded is 40-42 mph.

BULLDOZER

Hydraulic pistons control the angle of the blade and raise the blade

This dozer has a straight blade ("S blade") that is short and has no lateral curve and no side wings

The bulldozer blade is a heavy metal plate on the front of the tractor, used to push objects and shovel sand, soil and debris

TOP SPEED: 10 MPH

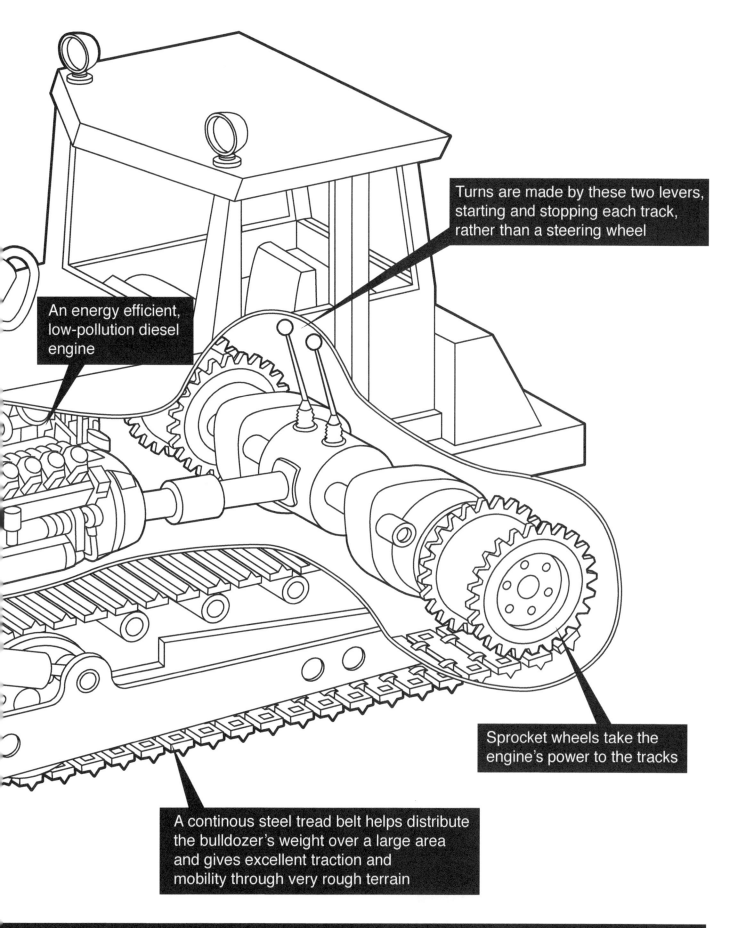

Turns are made by these two levers, starting and stopping each track, rather than a steering wheel

An energy efficient, low-pollution diesel engine

Sprocket wheels take the engine's power to the tracks

A continous steel tread belt helps distribute the bulldozer's weight over a large area and gives excellent traction and mobility through very rough terrain

A high-traction, earth-moving machine indispensible to building ponds, berms, or other earth-moving tasks such as building roads or clearing land.

A CEMENT TRUCK

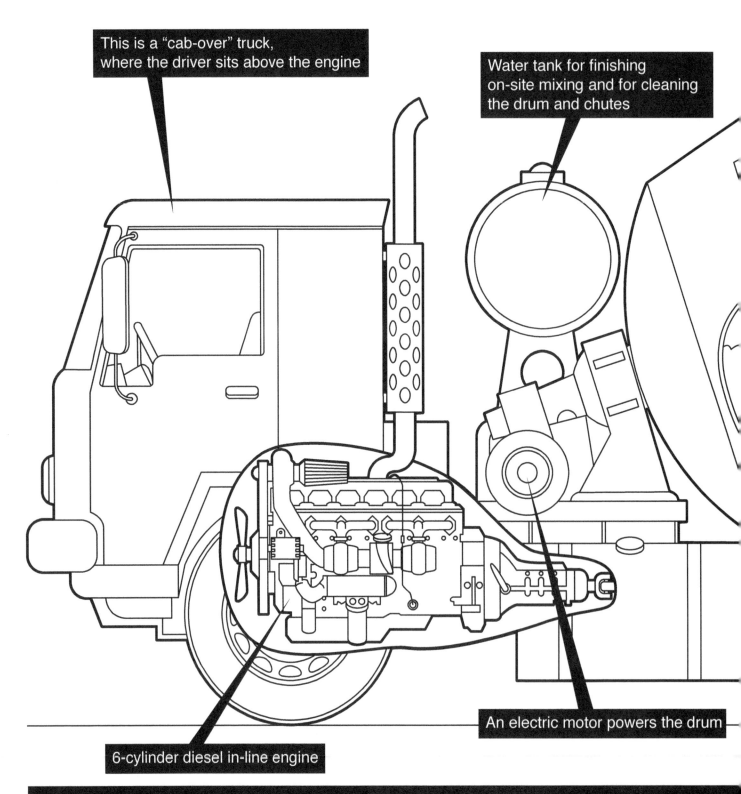

This is a "cab-over" truck, where the driver sits above the engine

Water tank for finishing on-site mixing and for cleaning the drum and chutes

An electric motor powers the drum

6-cylinder diesel in-line engine

READY-MIXED CONCRETE

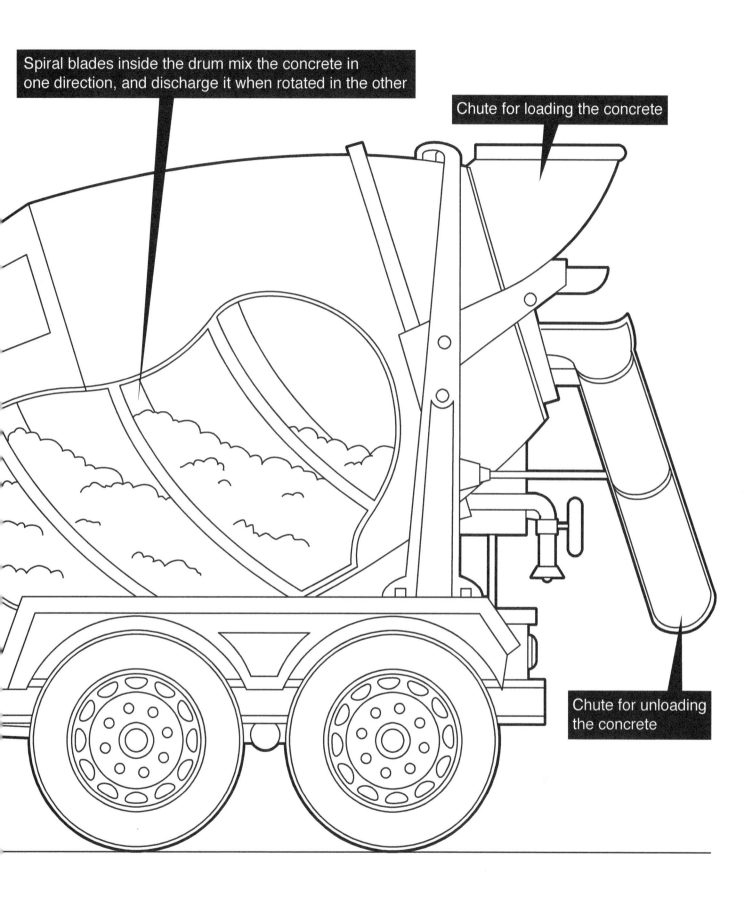

Spiral blades inside the drum mix the concrete in one direction, and discharge it when rotated in the other

Chute for loading the concrete

Chute for unloading the concrete

Each truckload of pre-mixed concrete must be unloaded within 90 minutes or 300 rotations or it will begin to harden.

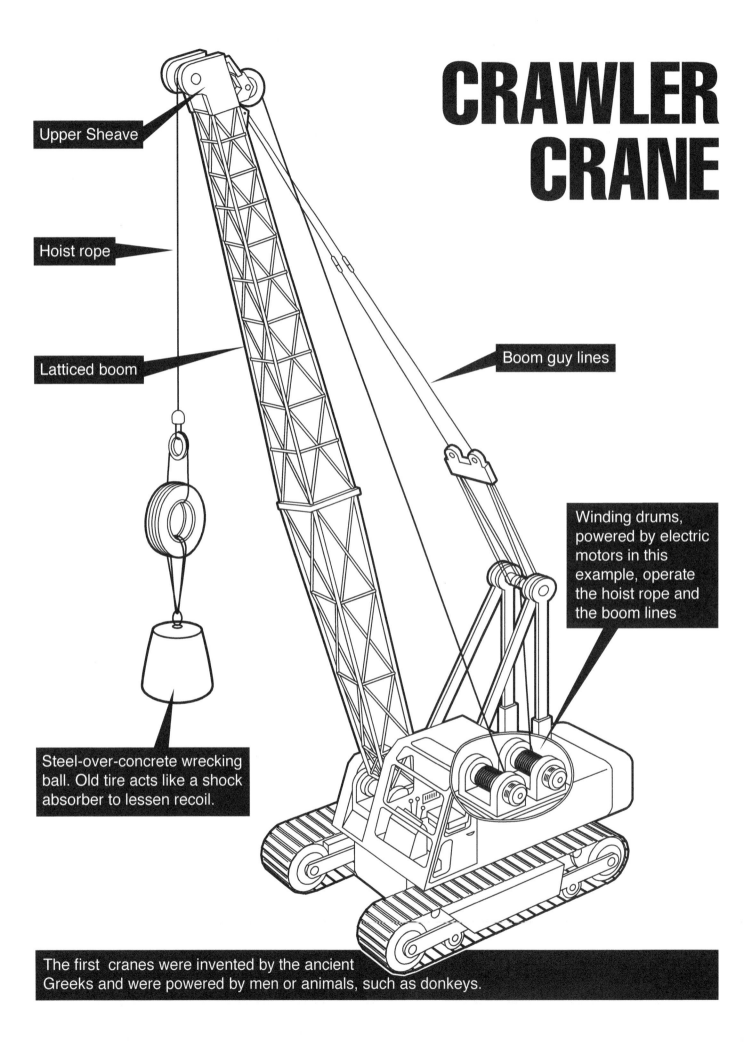

CRAWLER CRANE

Upper Sheave

Hoist rope

Latticed boom

Boom guy lines

Winding drums, powered by electric motors in this example, operate the hoist rope and the boom lines

Steel-over-concrete wrecking ball. Old tire acts like a shock absorber to lessen recoil.

The first cranes were invented by the ancient Greeks and were powered by men or animals, such as donkeys.

FORKLIFT

A chain drive pulls the fork, and whatever it holds, up and down

The lifting fork rides on a frame that slides inside the base body

Heavy steel weights are placed in the back of the forklift to counterbalance the weight of the items on the fork

The base body holds the chain drive motor

Hydraulic pistons control the angle of the lift frame

The engine powers the front wheels

Steering is done with the rear wheels

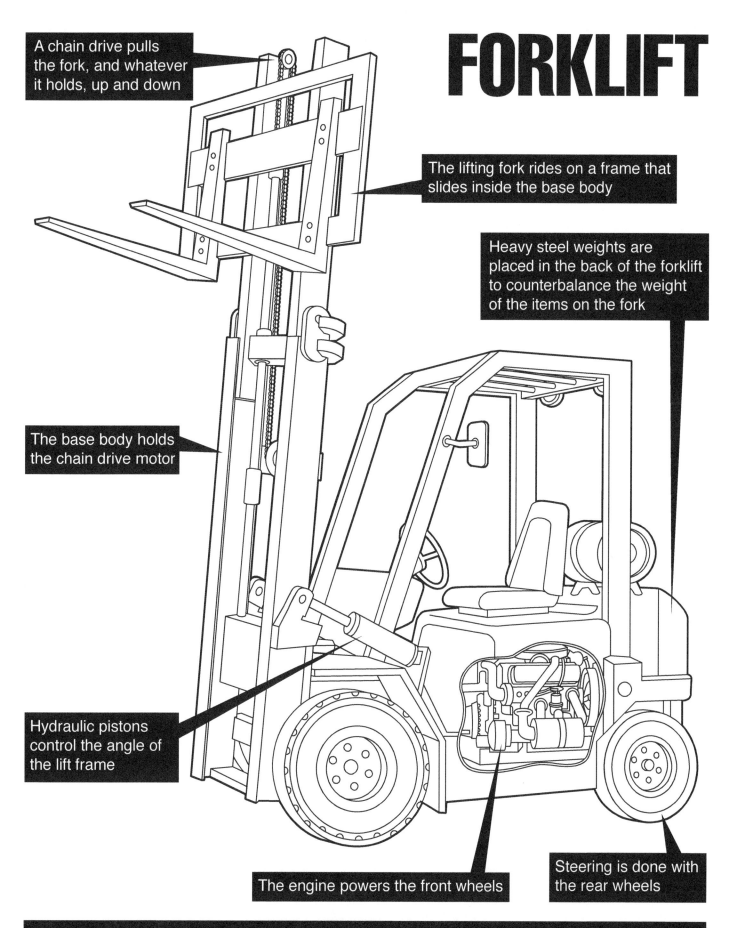

There are many different designs of forklifts, some electric and some with combustion engines. This propane example uses the basic chain drive and hydraulic cylinders to do the lifting.

CRUISE SHIP

Elevator banks allow easy access to other locations on different deck levels

Rear lounges and swimming pools

Outside dining and dancing

A propeller that can swivel 360 degrees makes this ship very maneuverable

Cabins for high-class travelers have balconies facing the water

Stabilizers keep the ship from rolling, so the passengers are less likely to get "sea-sick"

VACATIONING ON THE WATER

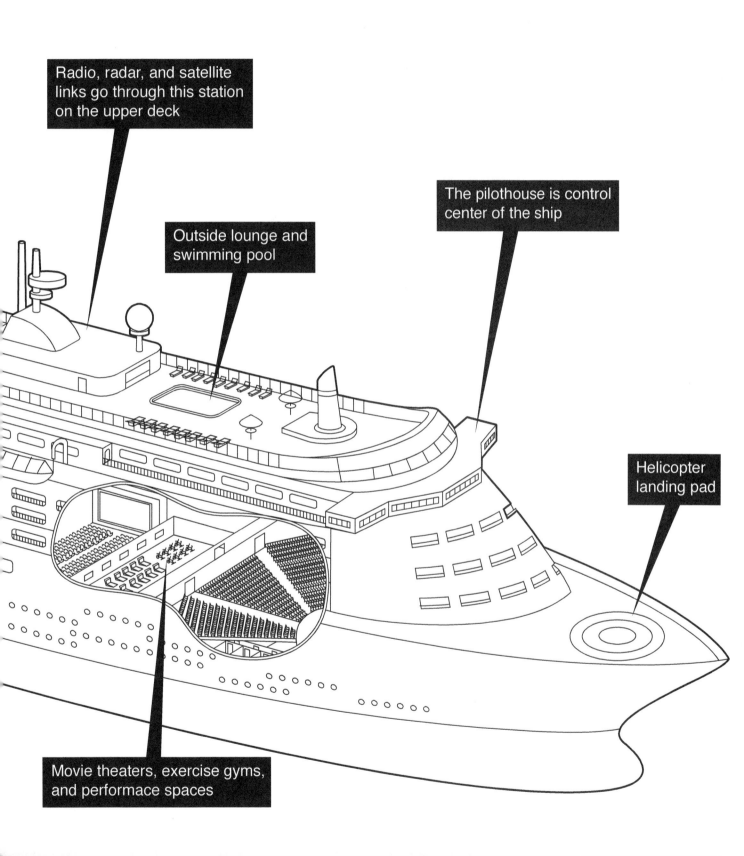

Radio, radar, and satellite links go through this station on the upper deck

Outside lounge and swimming pool

The pilothouse is control center of the ship

Helicopter landing pad

Movie theaters, exercise gyms, and performace spaces

Originally called "Ocean Liners," these large transporters, now called "Cruise Ships," have evolved into floating cities - where getting there is more than half the fun.

DIESEL- ELECTRIC TRAIN

V-16 diesel motor drives an electric alternator

Blower fans to cool the electric motors and brake units

Driver controls are at both ends of engine

Air cushion shock absorbers

A POWERHOUSE OF TRANSPORT

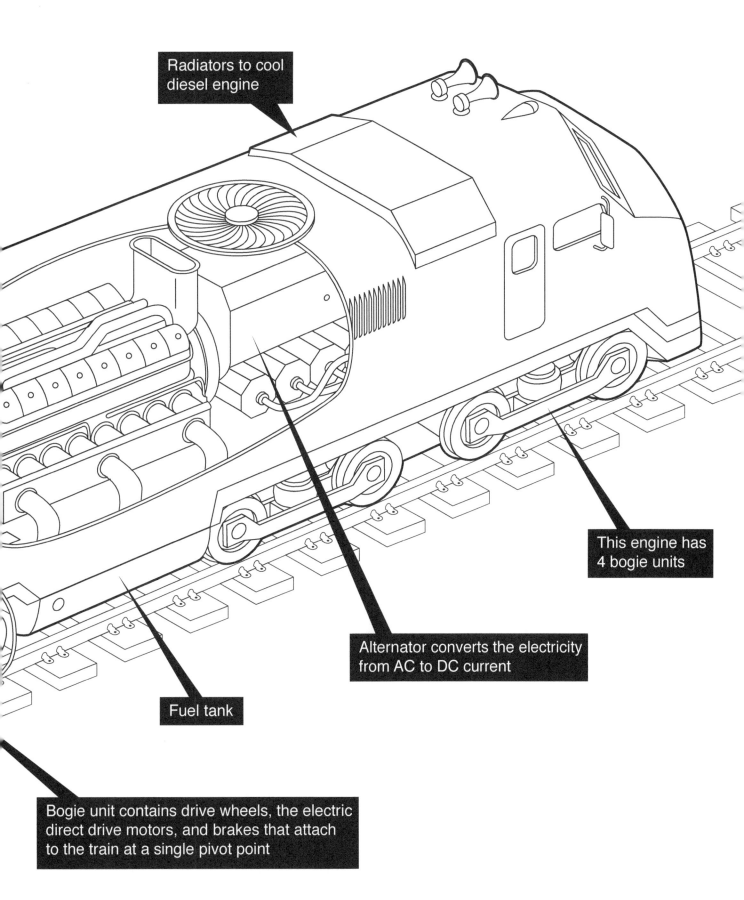

Radiators to cool
diesel engine

This engine has
4 bogie units

Alternator converts the electricity
from AC to DC current

Fuel tank

Bogie unit contains drive wheels, the electric
direct drive motors, and brakes that attach
to the train at a single pivot point

Modern locomotives are capable of pulling trains weighing in excess of 15,000 tons,
even going uphill.

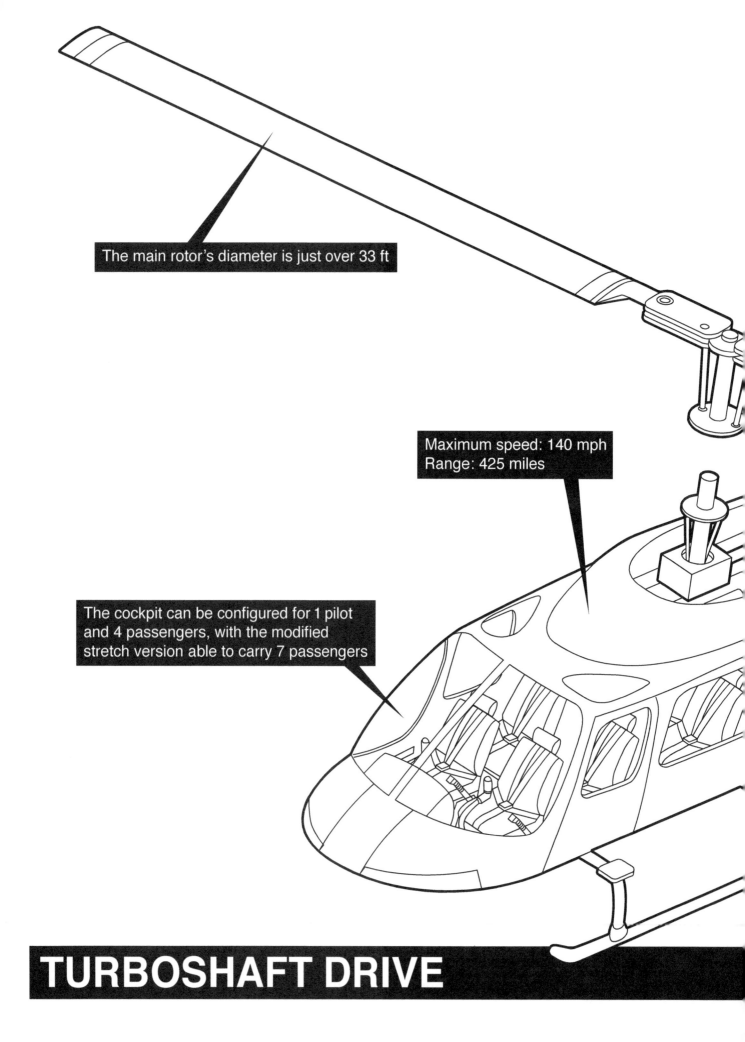

The main rotor's diameter is just over 33 ft

Maximum speed: 140 mph
Range: 425 miles

The cockpit can be configured for 1 pilot and 4 passengers, with the modified stretch version able to carry 7 passengers

TURBOSHAFT DRIVE

HELICOPTER

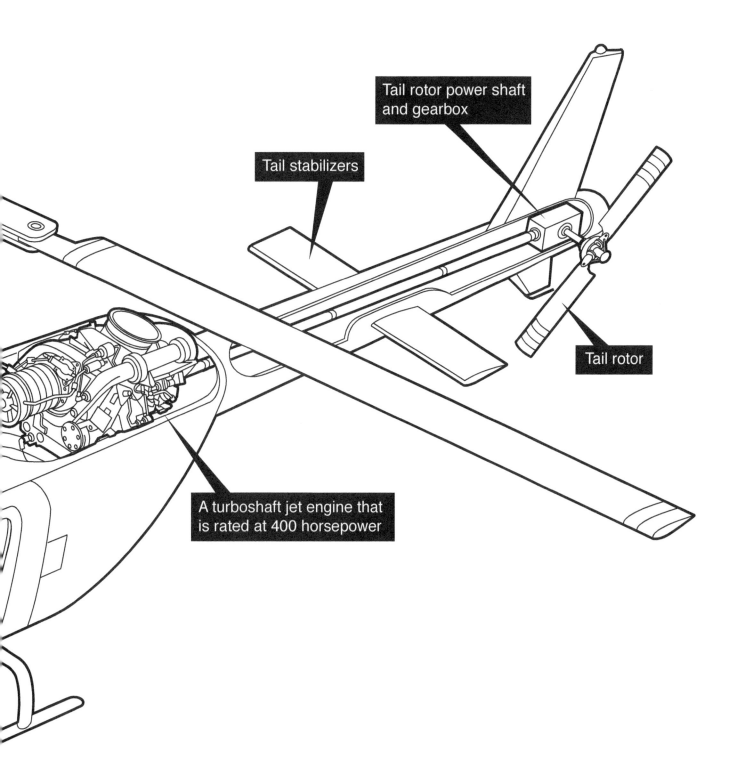

Tail rotor power shaft and gearbox

Tail stabilizers

Tail rotor

A turboshaft jet engine that is rated at 400 horsepower

This style of personal and small business helicopter with a single main rotor with anti-torque tail rotor configuration has become the world's most common design.

HOVERCRAFT

A single-seat sport model is shown to best display the essentail parts that makes this machine function

Flexible skirt of fabric and rubber act as suspension to allow the craft to float over rough surfaces

Throttle and steering stick are the two major control features

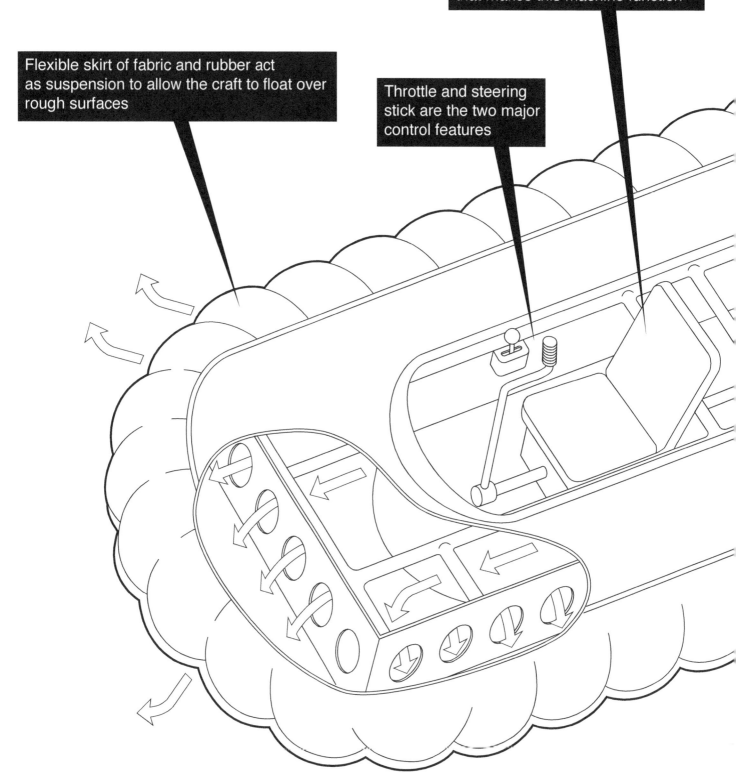

FLOATING ON AIR

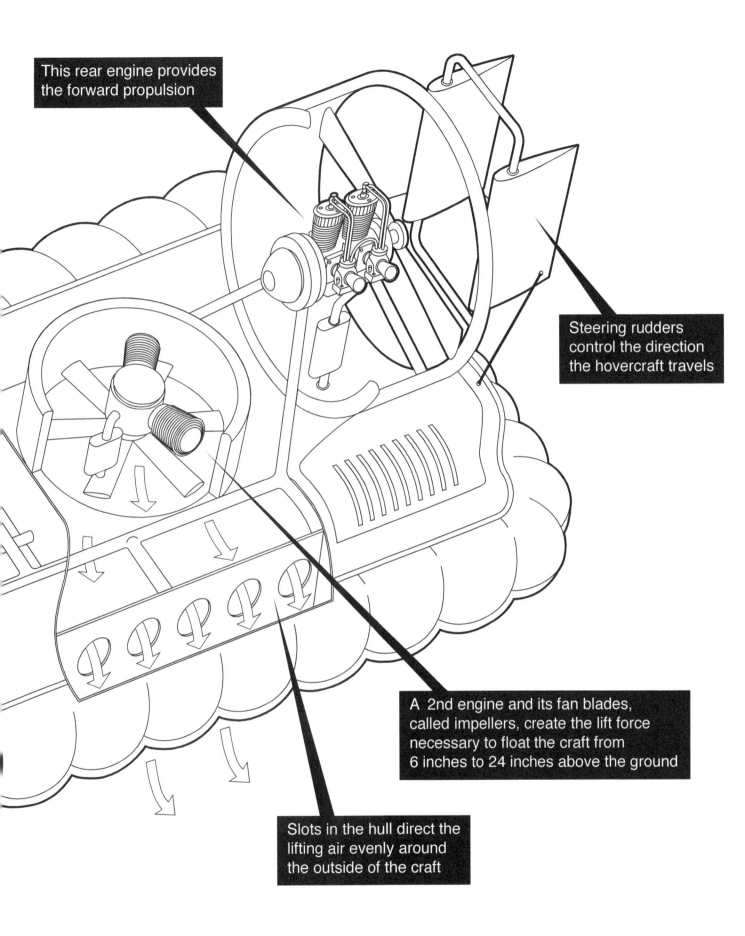

This rear engine provides the forward propulsion

Steering rudders control the direction the hovercraft travels

A 2nd engine and its fan blades, called impellers, create the lift force necessary to float the craft from 6 inches to 24 inches above the ground

Slots in the hull direct the lifting air evenly around the outside of the craft

Used throughout the world in military, sport or passenger transport. Large versions are daily used to ferry hundreds of people and vehicles across the English Channel.

HYBRID CAR

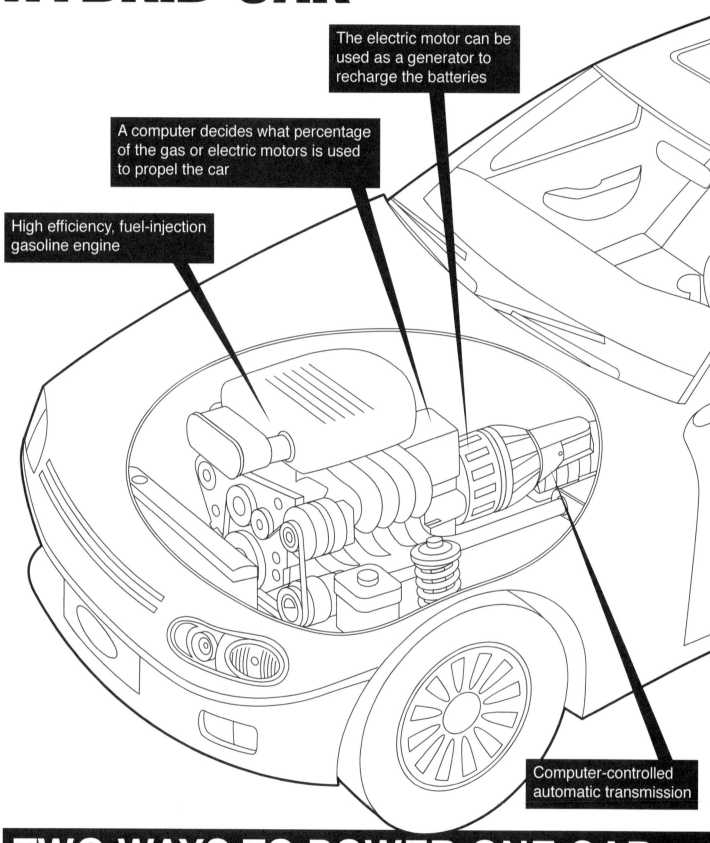

The electric motor can be used as a generator to recharge the batteries

A computer decides what percentage of the gas or electric motors is used to propel the car

High efficiency, fuel-injection gasoline engine

Computer-controlled automatic transmission

TWO WAYS TO POWER ONE CAR

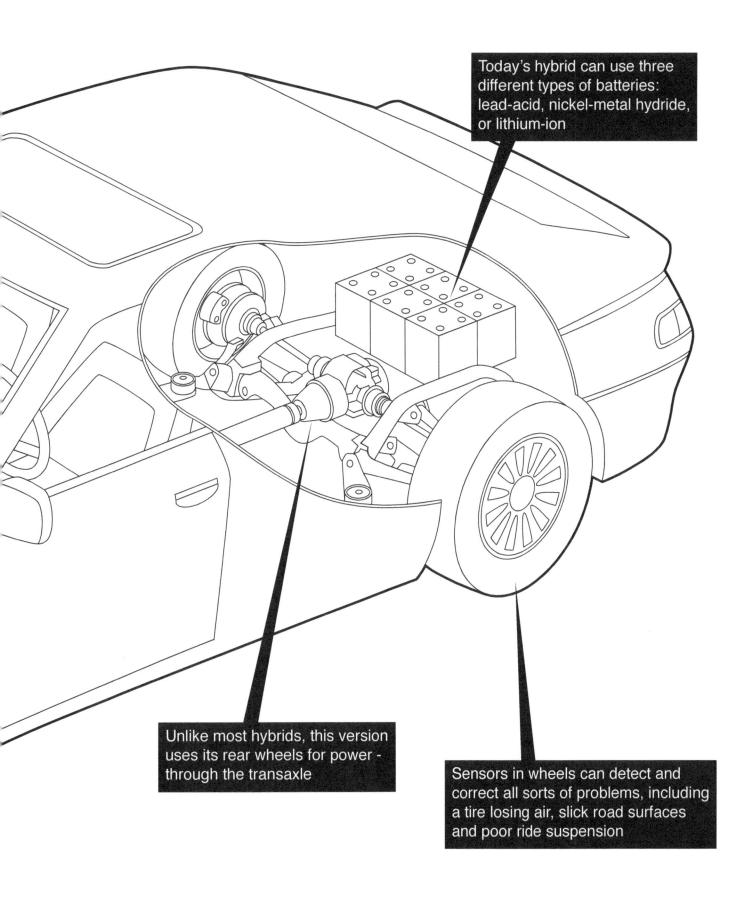

Today's hybrid can use three different types of batteries: lead-acid, nickel-metal hydride, or lithium-ion

Unlike most hybrids, this version uses its rear wheels for power - through the transaxle

Sensors in wheels can detect and correct all sorts of problems, including a tire losing air, slick road surfaces and poor ride suspension

This is a power-split hybrid electric vehicle - powered by either the gas or electric motor, or both at the same time. The gas engine automatically switches off when the car is motionless.

JET AIRLINER

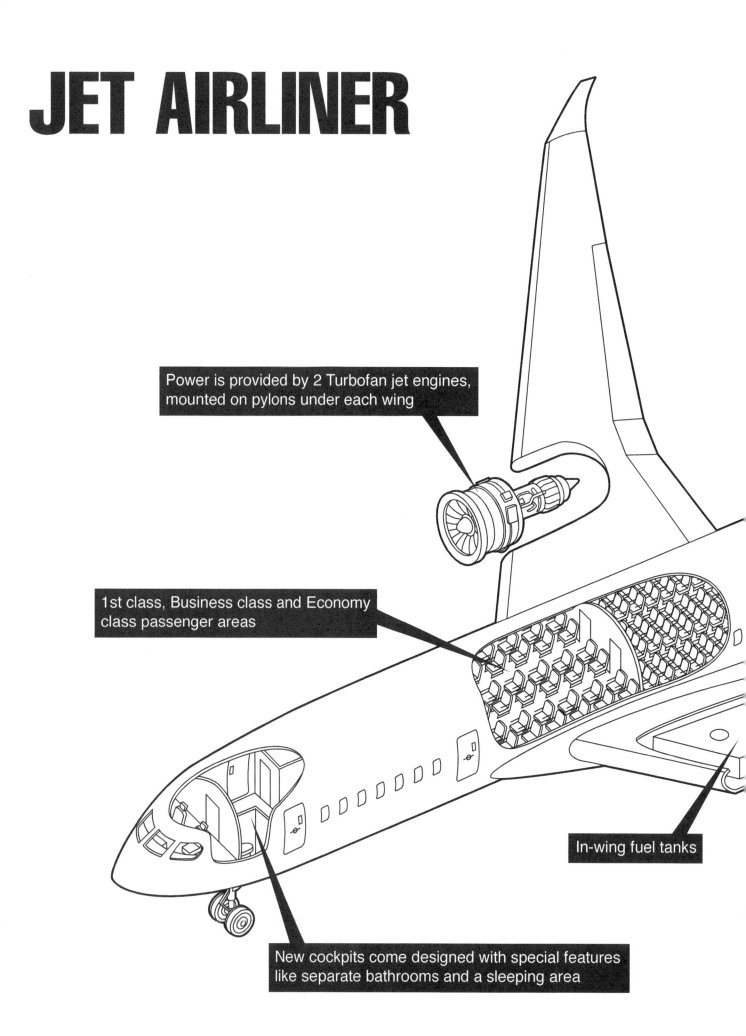

Power is provided by 2 Turbofan jet engines, mounted on pylons under each wing

1st class, Business class and Economy class passenger areas

In-wing fuel tanks

New cockpits come designed with special features like separate bathrooms and a sleeping area

A TYPICAL MEDIUM-RANGE PASSENGER JET

Depending upon different company designs and interior layouts, these jets can carry 170 to 220 passengers 3,800 miles at a cruising speed of 550 mph.

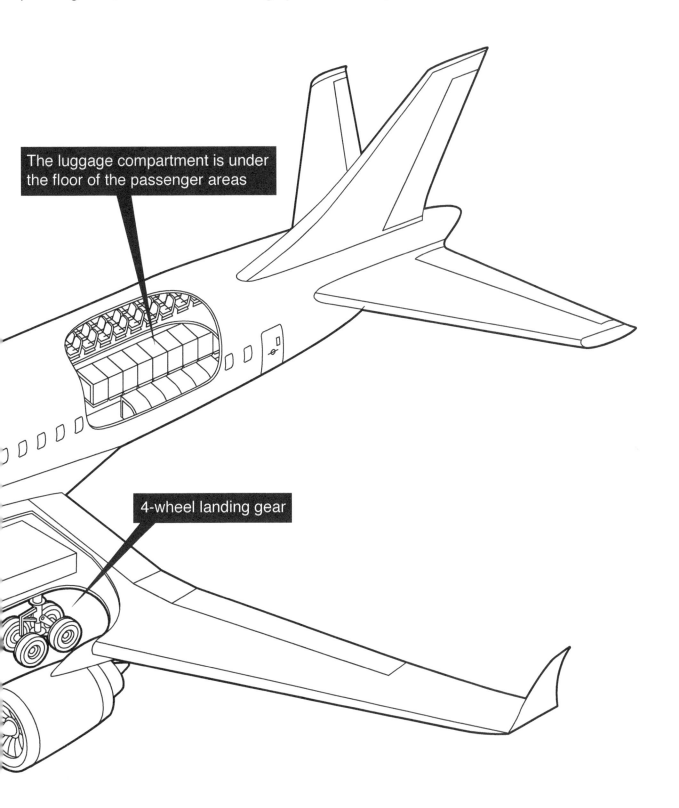

The luggage compartment is under the floor of the passenger areas

4-wheel landing gear

MONSTER TRUCK

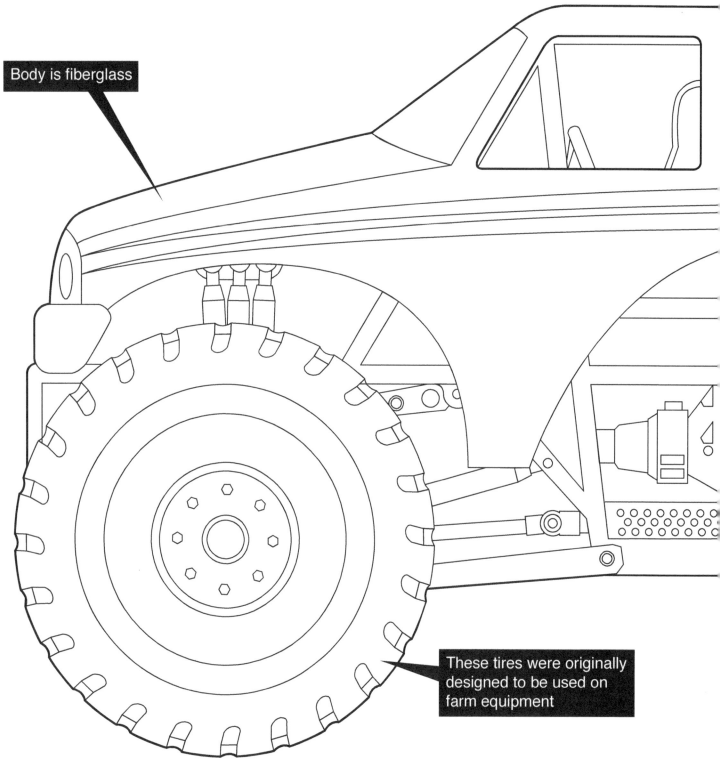

Body is fiberglass

These tires were originally designed to be used on farm equipment

CRUSHING CARS SINCE 1981

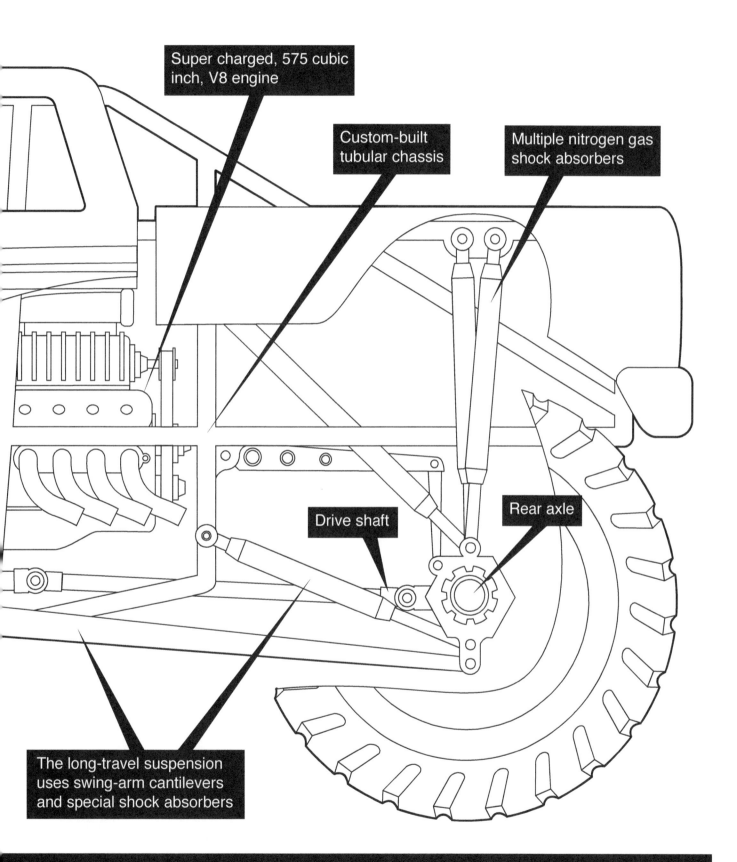

Super charged, 575 cubic inch, V8 engine

Custom-built tubular chassis

Multiple nitrogen gas shock absorbers

Drive shaft

Rear axle

The long-travel suspension uses swing-arm cantilevers and special shock absorbers

The monster truck has evolved from a modified standard pickup to a hand-built machine, capable of leaps, speed, and tricks that amaze and please arena-sized crowds.

MOTORCYCLE

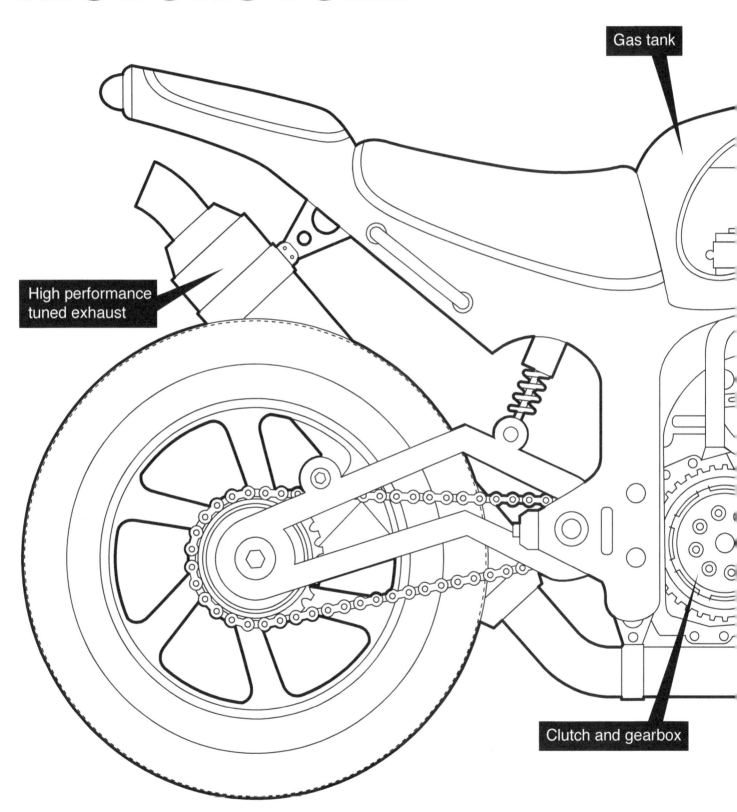

Gas tank

High performance
tuned exhaust

Clutch and gearbox

A SPORT BIKE

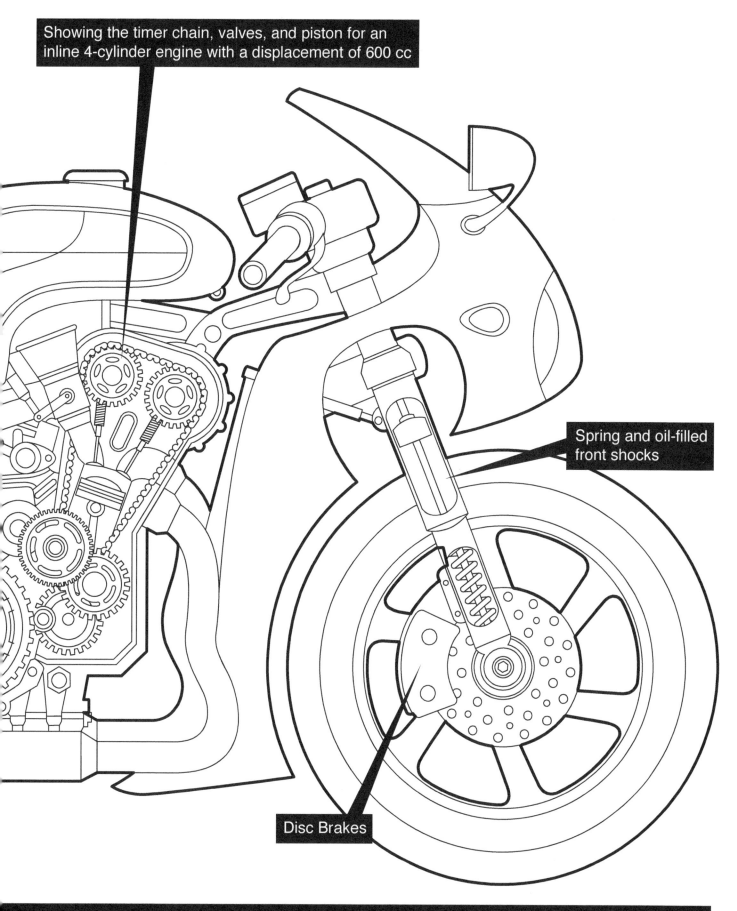

Showing the timer chain, valves, and piston for an inline 4-cylinder engine with a displacement of 600 cc

Spring and oil-filled front shocks

Disc Brakes

Designed for street-riding performance, sport bikes are characterized by powerful engines, responsive handling, and arms-forward posture.

PERSONAL WATER CRAFT

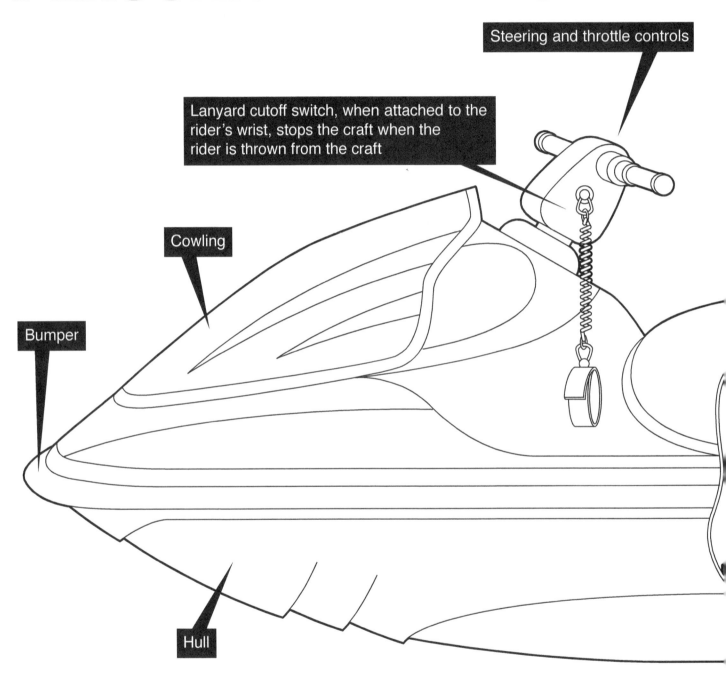

Steering and throttle controls

Lanyard cutoff switch, when attached to the rider's wrist, stops the craft when the rider is thrown from the craft

Cowling

Bumper

Hull

A TYPICAL WATER SCOOTER

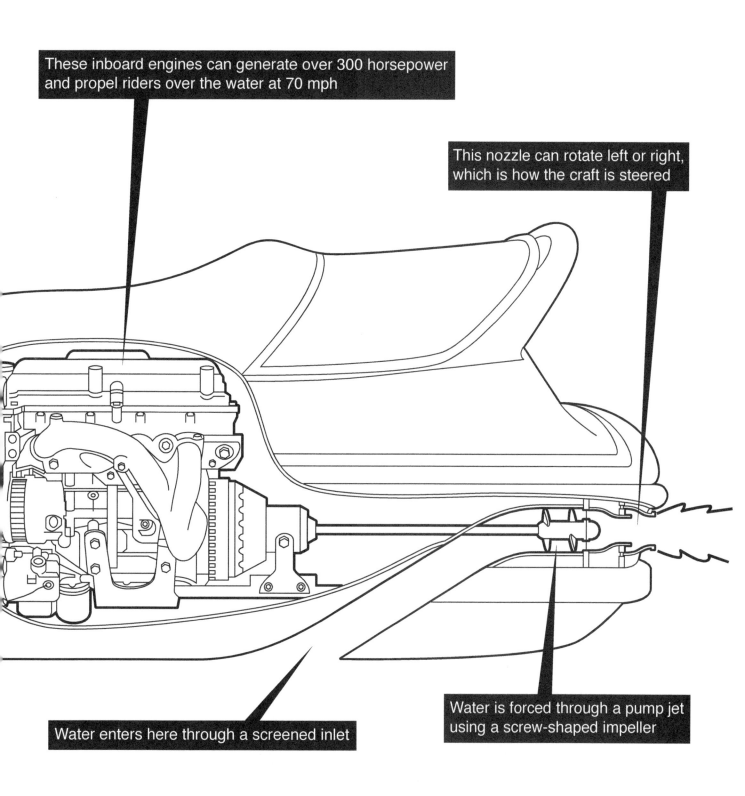

These inboard engines can generate over 300 horsepower and propel riders over the water at 70 mph

This nozzle can rotate left or right, which is how the craft is steered

Water is forced through a pump jet using a screw-shaped impeller

Water enters here through a screened inlet

A recreational watercraft that the rider rides or stands on and can carry as many as 4 passengers. The "first commercially successful" watercraft was released by the Kawasaki company in 1972.

ROAD ROLLER

With two steering wheels and a driver's seat that can be swiveled 180 degrees, the operator has an excellent view of the work area for best results and safety

Road rollers can have many different designs; this set-up of two full-width rollers is called a "Duplex"

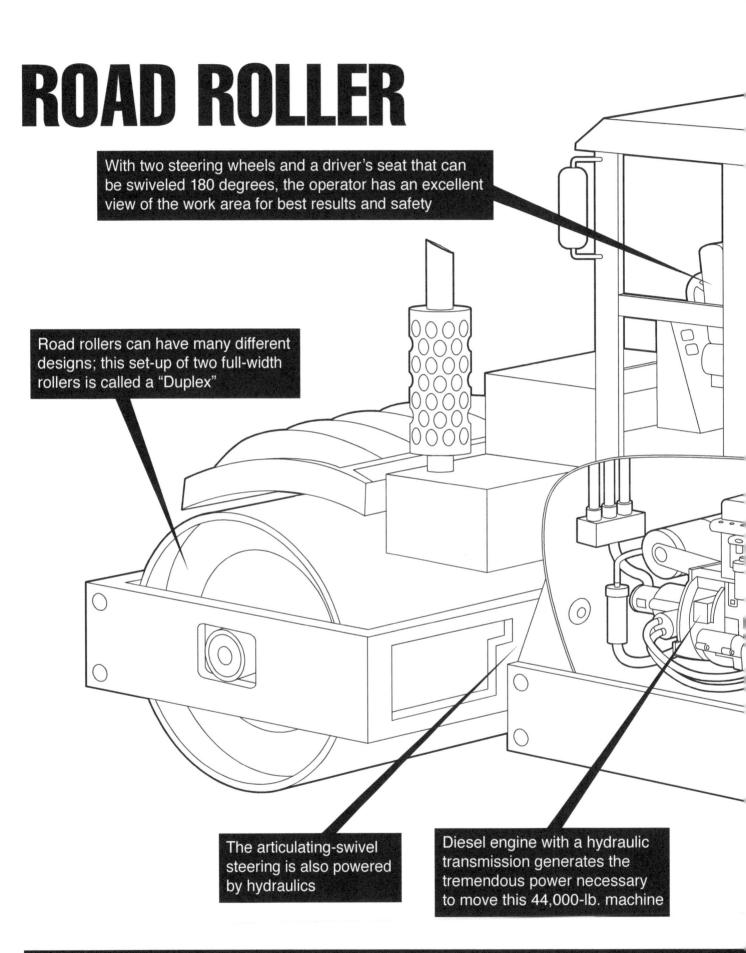

The articulating-swivel steering is also powered by hydraulics

Diesel engine with a hydraulic transmission generates the tremendous power necessary to move this 44,000-lb. machine

MAKING THE ROAD SMOOTH

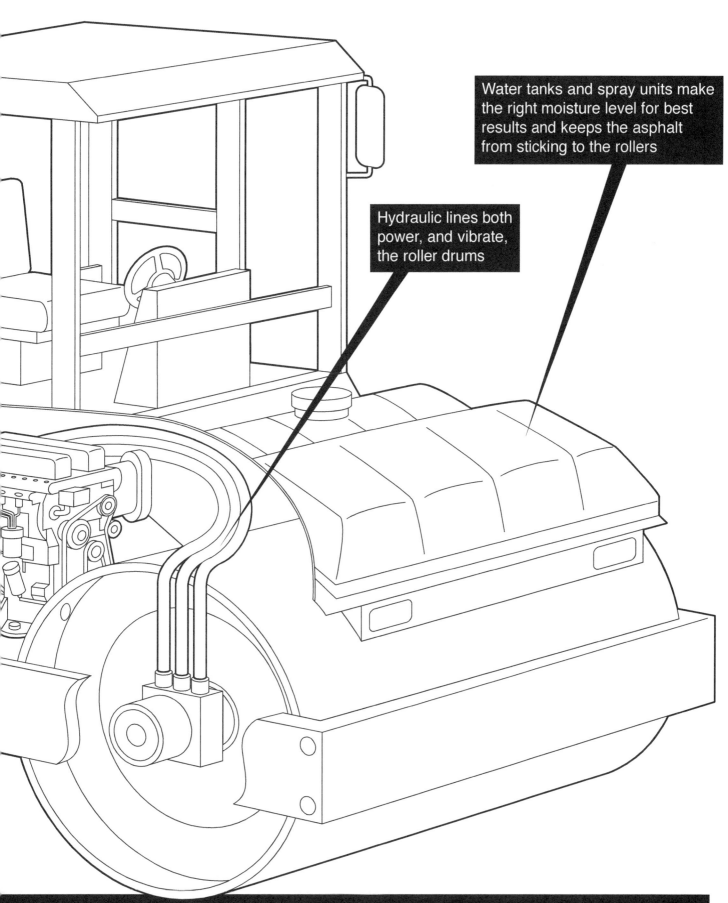

Water tanks and spray units make the right moisture level for best results and keeps the asphalt from sticking to the rollers

Hydraulic lines both power, and vibrate, the roller drums

The roller drums may be filled with water on site to achieve the desired weight. When empty, the lighter machine is much easier and cheaper to transport.

ROCKET TO SPACE

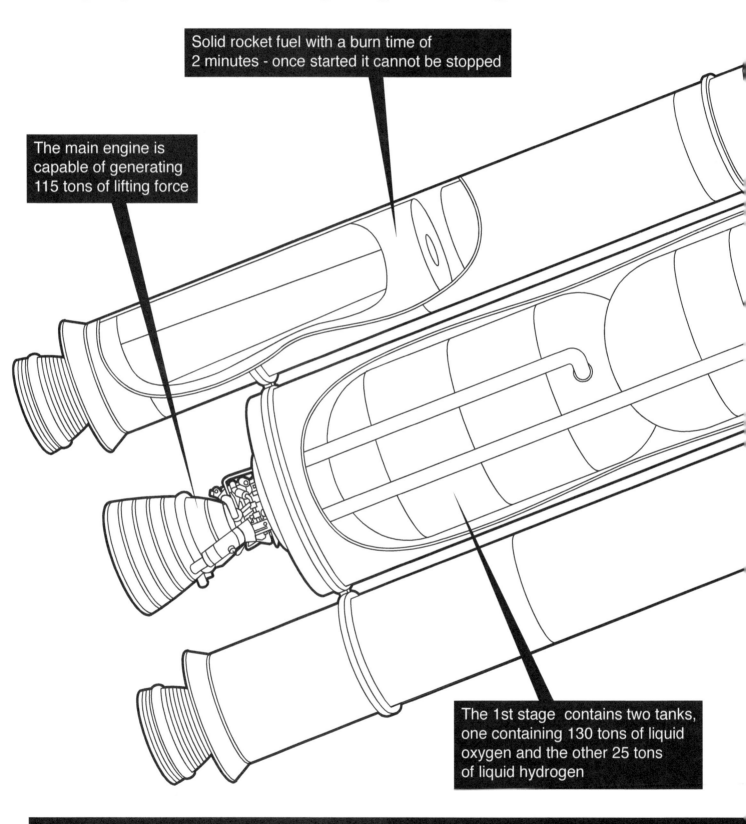

Solid rocket fuel with a burn time of 2 minutes - once started it cannot be stopped

The main engine is capable of generating 115 tons of lifting force

The 1st stage contains two tanks, one containing 130 tons of liquid oxygen and the other 25 tons of liquid hydrogen

A COMMERCIAL ROCKET

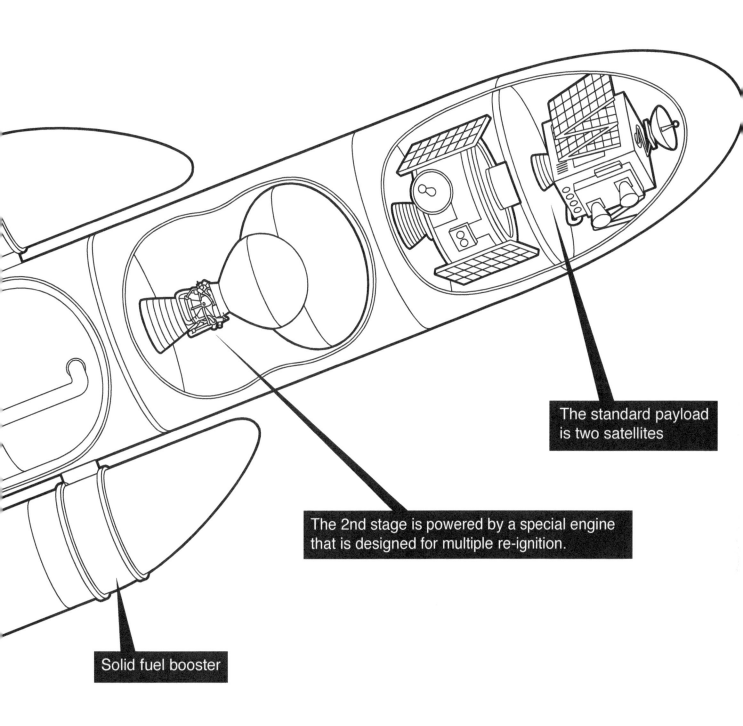

The standard payload is two satellites

The 2nd stage is powered by a special engine that is designed for multiple re-ignition.

Solid fuel booster

Developed by a European group, this two-stage launcher uses both liquid rocket motors and non-reusable strap-on boosters using solid propellant.

RV FUN

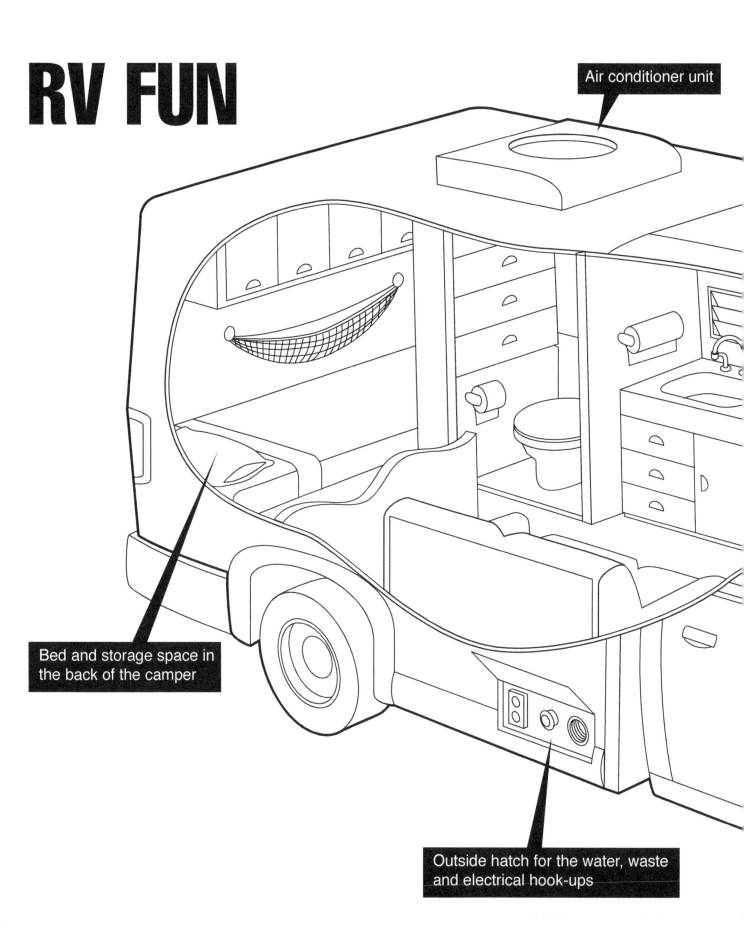

Air conditioner unit

Bed and storage space in the back of the camper

Outside hatch for the water, waste and electrical hook-ups

A CAMPER CONVERSION

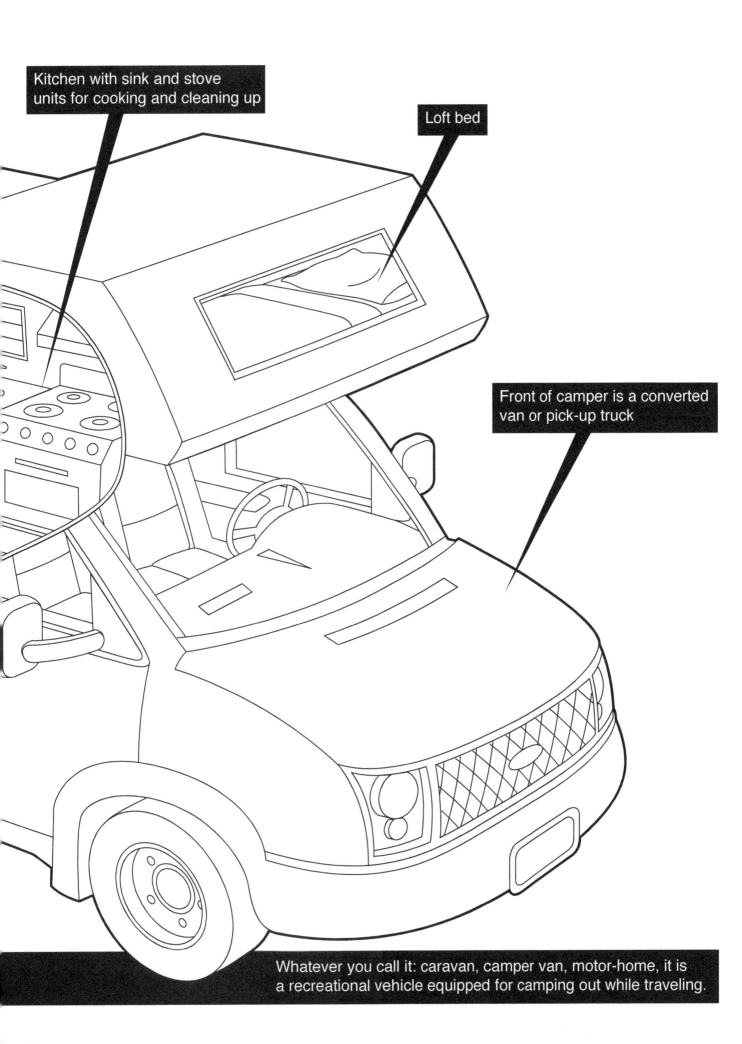

Kitchen with sink and stove units for cooking and cleaning up

Loft bed

Front of camper is a converted van or pick-up truck

Whatever you call it: caravan, camper van, motor-home, it is a recreational vehicle equipped for camping out while traveling.

SNOWMOBILE

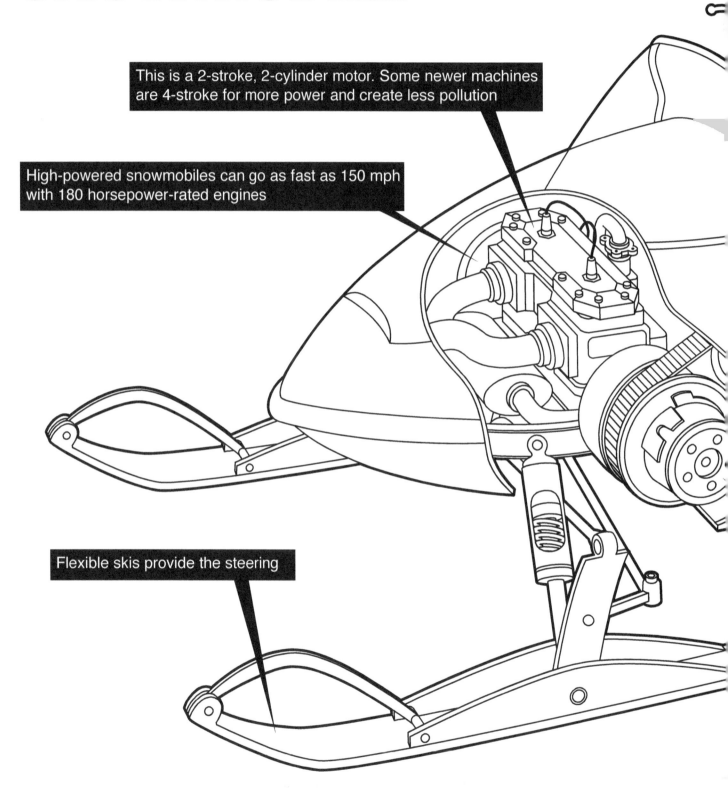

This is a 2-stroke, 2-cylinder motor. Some newer machines are 4-stroke for more power and create less pollution

High-powered snowmobiles can go as fast as 150 mph with 180 horsepower-rated engines

Flexible skis provide the steering

THE ALL-TERRAIN MACHINE FOR SNOW

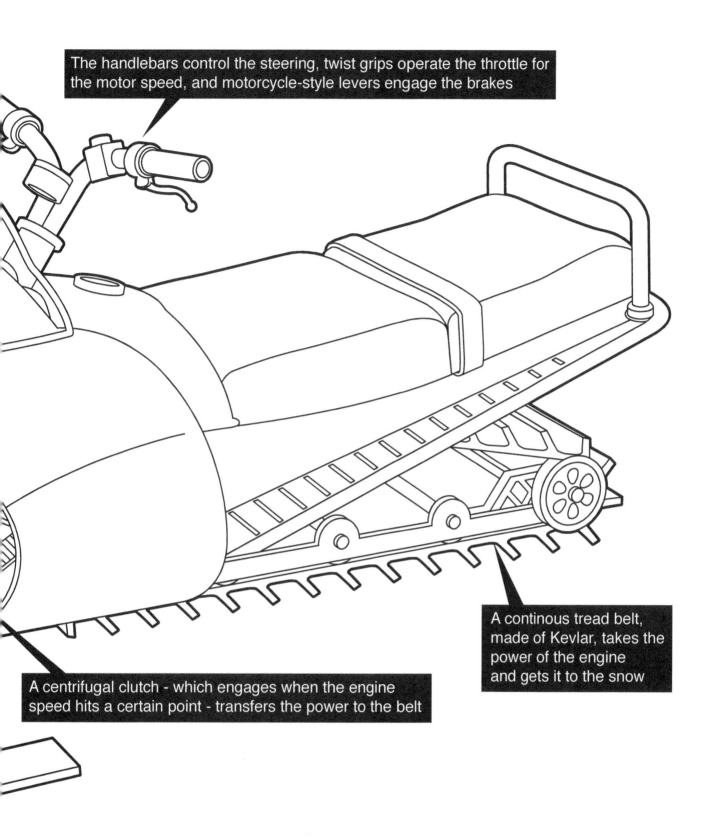

The handlebars control the steering, twist grips operate the throttle for the motor speed, and motorcycle-style levers engage the brakes

A continous tread belt, made of Kevlar, takes the power of the engine and gets it to the snow

A centrifugal clutch - which engages when the engine speed hits a certain point - transfers the power to the belt

In 1959, the first modern-designed snowmobile was sold. This style of snowmobile is the standard for 2-person transport in snowy regions as well as a popular recreation machine.

STREET SWEEPER

Water sprays keeps dust down and loosen particles

A CLEAN MACHINE

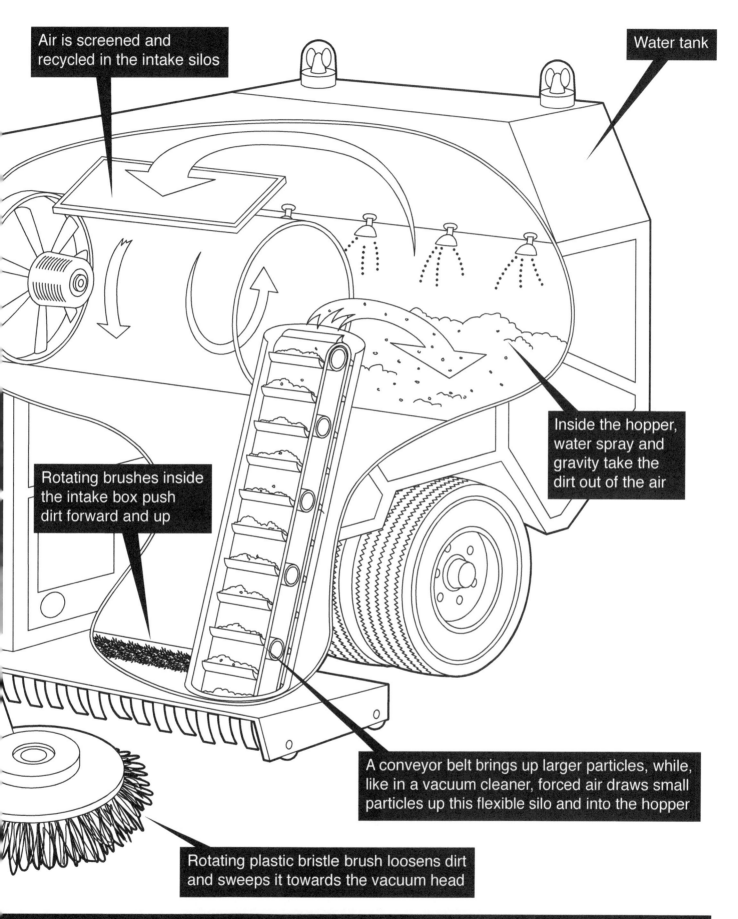

Air is screened and recycled in the intake silos

Water tank

Inside the hopper, water spray and gravity take the dirt out of the air

Rotating brushes inside the intake box push dirt forward and up

A conveyor belt brings up larger particles, while, like in a vacuum cleaner, forced air draws small particles up this flexible silo and into the hopper

Rotating plastic bristle brush loosens dirt and sweeps it towards the vacuum head

The Environmental Protection Agency considers street sweeping a Best Management Practice in protecting water quality.

SUBMARINE

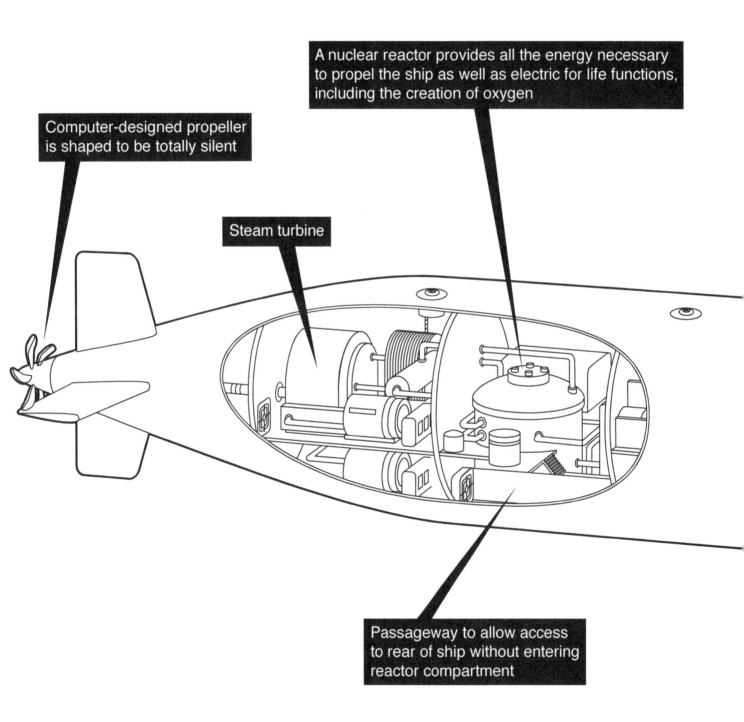

A nuclear reactor provides all the energy necessary to propel the ship as well as electric for life functions, including the creation of oxygen

Computer-designed propeller is shaped to be totally silent

Steam turbine

Passageway to allow access to rear of ship without entering reactor compartment

NUCLEAR ATTACK SUBMARINE

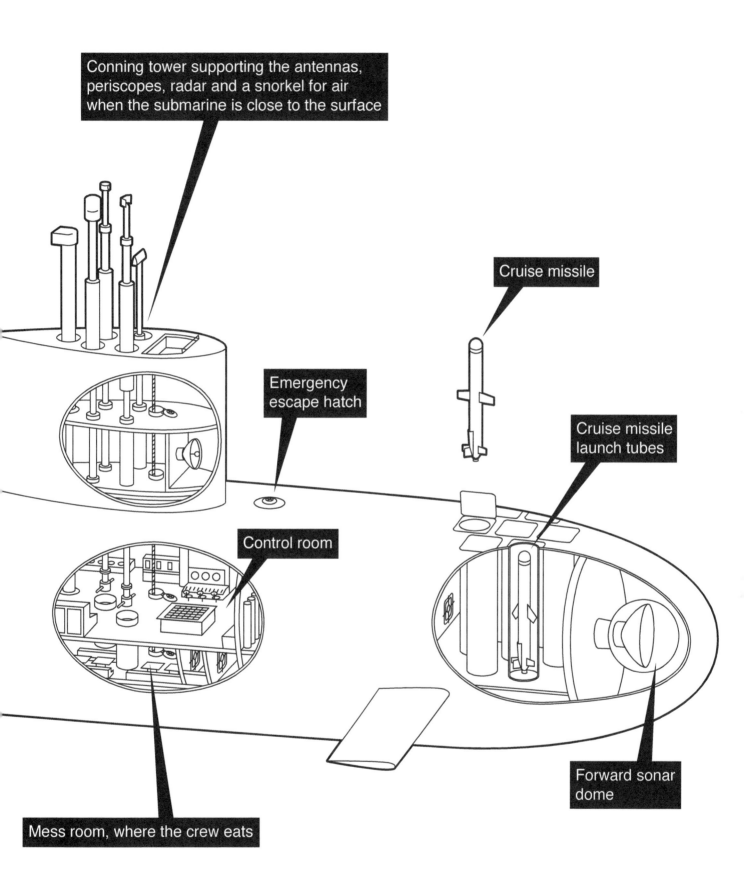

Conning tower supporting the antennas, periscopes, radar and a snorkel for air when the submarine is close to the surface

Cruise missile

Emergency escape hatch

Cruise missile launch tubes

Control room

Forward sonar dome

Mess room, where the crew eats

Able to stay submerged for long periods, this generalized example shows the major elements that make these vessels the most important member of a naval fleet.

SAILBOAT

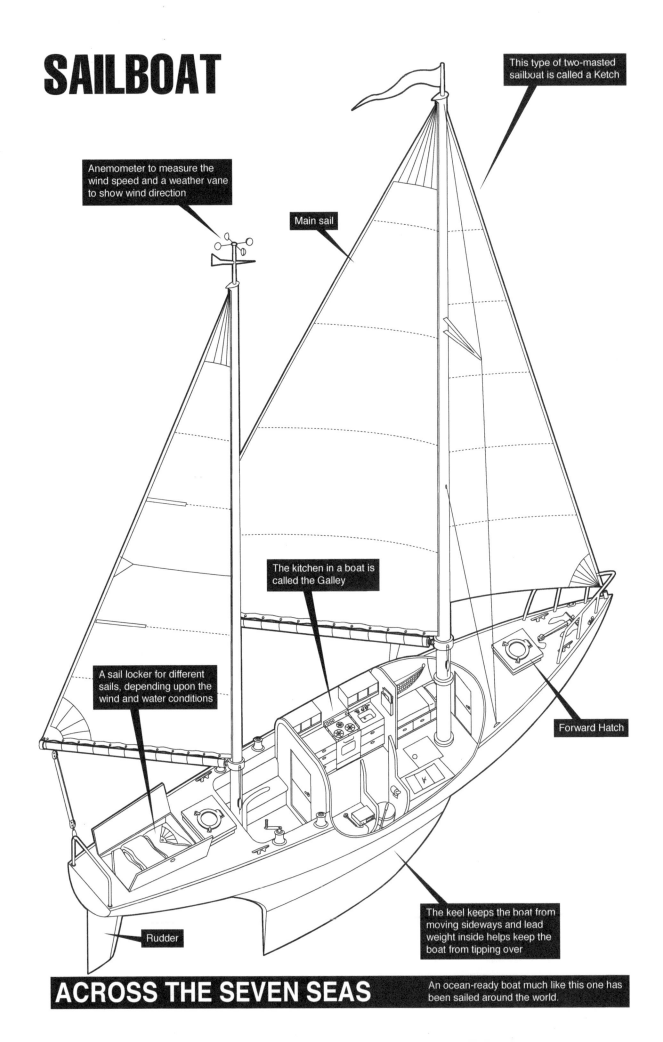

This type of two-masted sailboat is called a Ketch

Anemometer to measure the wind speed and a weather vane to show wind direction

Main sail

The kitchen in a boat is called the Galley

A sail locker for different sails, depending upon the wind and water conditions

Forward Hatch

Rudder

The keel keeps the boat from moving sideways and lead weight inside helps keep the boat from tipping over

ACROSS THE SEVEN SEAS

An ocean-ready boat much like this one has been sailed around the world.